PROJECT-BASED LEARNING IN SCIENCE™

EXPLORING CONTROLLED INVESTIGATIONS THROUGH SCIENCE RESEARCH PROJECTS

ANGIE TIMMONS

rosen publishing's rosen central®
New York

Published in 2019 by The Rosen Publishing Group, Inc.
29 East 21st Street, New York, NY 10010

First Edition

Library of Congress Cataloging-in-Publication Data

Names: Timmons, Angie, author.
Title: Exploring controlled investigations through science research projects / Angie Timmons.
Description: First edition. | New York: Rosen Central, 2019. | Series: Project-based learning in science | Audience: Grades 5–8. | Includes bibliographical references and index.
Identifiers: LCCN 2018014359| ISBN 9781508184720 (library bound) | ISBN 9781508184713 (pbk.)
Subjects: LCSH: Science—Study and teaching—Activity programs. | Science projects—Juvenile literature. | Student-centered learning—Juvenile literature. | Project method in teaching—Juvenile literature.
Classification: LCC Q164 .T56 2019 | DDC 507.8—dc23
LC record available at https://lccn.loc.gov/2018014359

Manufactured in the United States of America

CONTENTS

INTRODUCTION

In December 2017, National Geographic footage of a polar bear on Canada's Baffin Island went viral. The heart-wrenching video showed a weak and starving polar bear struggling to stay upright. Viewers could see how global warming, a dangerous environmental phenomenon, had impacted the environment: melting ice had led to a compromised environment in which the bear could not survive. By the time the footage went viral, some experts theorized the bear had likely already died. For decades, scientists and environmentalists have warned that global warming must be stopped; however, humankind has persisted in increasing industrialization and other practices that produce pollutants and contribute to irreversible climate change. The devastating and cruel impact of human-made climate change on creatures unable to protect themselves was clear in the polar bear video.

People are victims of climate change, too. In August 2005, Hurricane Katrina hit the southeastern United States with such devastating force that some communities in states like Mississippi and Louisiana still haven't fully recovered. Millions of people were left homeless; more than eighteen hundred died; and between damages and other costs, Katrina was the costliest hurricane in US history at $241 billion. Everyone from scientists to humanitarians to common citizens pleaded for policies requiring more responsible practices to decrease global warming, which is a major factor in causing more frequent and severe hurricanes. We've failed to make progress: Hurricanes Harvey and Irma hit the Caribbean and states like Texas and Florida in quick succession in August and September 2017. Harvey caused a combined $175 billion in damages. Harvey and Irma displaced thousands of people and killed 222.

We need young scientists who will take the helm in studying and finding solutions to problems like climate change. Project-based learning, or PBL, is a great way to start your scientific journey. Although science is a hands-on topic, traditional teaching methods don't allow learners to experience science for themselves. PBL puts students in charge of how they learn by allowing them to engage through investigation, collaboration, decision making, problem solving, reflection, and presentation to peers and teachers. In fact, readers should not feel limited to the projects in this book but instead feel free to take these projects as models with which to design their own investigations. In PBL, learners should frame projects in a real-world context by tying topics to current issues or problems—like the increase in hurricanes or the plight of starving polar bears.

One of the most hands-on types of PBL projects is a controlled investigation. In a controlled investigation, scientists (or students) perform an experiment in which they manipulate, or change, one or more variables. The term "variable" just means something that can change. Controlled experiments involve a controlled group (often just called a control) that sets a standard against which the experimental group can be measured. The experimental group gets exposed to an independent variable—which can be anything, such as loud noises, toxic chemicals, or an experimental medicine—to test what effect that variable has.

In project-based learning, you'll work with classmates, technology, and scientific tools—like the students in this photo, using test tubes to study plant life—to understand concepts.

Project-based learning encourages students to use technology. As learners carry out their controlled investigations using PBL, they should identify an array of technology-based ways to find, store, and organize their research and to design their final presentation.

While science is complex and can be intimidating, it's also fascinating. Whether simply studying the conditions needed to grow a plant or engineering a mechanical device, learners will find, through PBL, that science's major disciplines connect not only with each other but with our everyday lives. PBL makes science less intimidating by putting students in charge of how they learn.

CHAPTER ONE

PHYSICAL SCIENCE

Have you ever wondered how a roller coaster can move at high speeds, swerve all around, turn upside down, and take its passengers on a seemingly impossible, thrilling ride? The answer is physical science, the science of energy and matter. Matter is almost everything we encounter in our world, both seen and unseen, like soil and air. Energy is universal and gives matter the ability to move and transform. Energy can be seen at work in things like electricity, heat, and light.

A moving roller coaster subjects matter, such as the riders and the carts they ride in, to strong forces such as gravity, magnetic conduction, and velocity. A roller coaster is started by a motor, which is a process that uses energy. Matter, other types of energy, and the application of sciences like physics and chemistry do the rest.

VARIABLES IN CONTROLLED INVESTIGATIONS

Controlled investigations involve several types of variables.

Independent variable: This variable helps experimenters answer questions. It is the variable that changes, and the effects of the changes are usually the subject of the experiment.

Controlled variables: These are the materials, measurements, and methods that need to stay exactly the same in every trial so that only independent variables can be held responsible for changes. Experiments can have several controlled variables.

Dependent variable: This is what changes as a result of the independent variables. Controlled investigations explore what happens (the dependent variable) because of what was changed (independent variable) compared to the controlled variable.

QUESTION: WHAT MAKES SOME THINGS MAGNETIC AND OTHERS NOT? ARE ALL METALS MAGNETIC?

We've all seen magnets stuck to refrigerators. Without glue, adhesive, or tape, they stay put, but how? Why don't we see magnets stuck to all kinds of other surfaces? The answer is magnetism, a physical phenomenon created by an electric charge that produces a magnetic field that will act on the electric currents of other objects. This charge results in either attractive (objects stick together) or repulsive (objects resist each other) forces between objects.

PROJECT
MAGNETISM

In this project, the group will learn more about magnetism, make predictions about magnetic items, test various items to determine magnetism, record data, and present findings.

- *Research magnetism and known magnetic materials, ferromagnetic materials, magnetic fields, magnetic conduction, electrons in magnetism, and magnetic poles. Form a hypothesis about what items will be magnetic based on your research.*
- *Make sure the teacher can provide a magnet that's appropriate for a science experiment—a magnet from a refrigerator won't work in this experiment. The magnet is a controlled variable, an item that stays the same throughout the experiment. Using the magnet and what the group has learned about magnetism and ferromagnetic materials, identify at least one known magnetic surface or material. This known material will be the control, because it's the one item the group knows attracts a magnet. Before the group begins testing the magnet against other materials, record the properties of the known material that the group found to be magnetic. These*

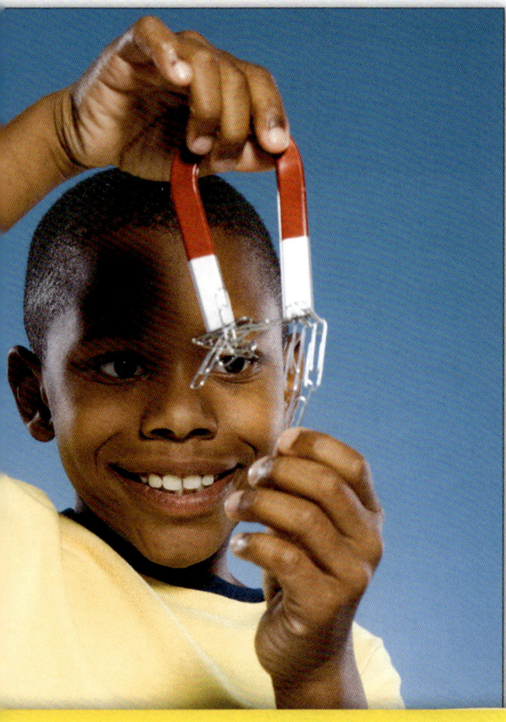

This student is experimenting with paper clips and a magnet to test their magnetic attraction. The kind of magnet he is holding is known as a horseshoe or U-shaped magnet.

properties will be important later, when the group compares this material to others tested.

- *Now, start testing the magnet on other items. These items will be the independent variables. Suggested items include an aluminum can, a copper penny, a metal key, a door handle, and other magnets. As the group tests the magnet against these items, record the findings as a list, naming each item, whether it's magnetic, and if anything interesting happens. For instance, what happened when the original magnet was placed against the other magnets?*
- *Now that the research and experiment are done, examine the findings. What properties did the magnetic materials display compared to the properties of the nonmagnetic materials? Was the magnet attracted to all*

metals? What roles do the north and south poles of magnets play?

- To present the findings to your class, make sure all the items used in the experiment are available for display to the class. Then, ask the group what makes something magnetic and what makes something not magnetic. Are all metals magnetic?
- Do a magnetism demonstration for your class. Show the interaction between magnet and control material. Then, show the class what happens when the other items you tested come in contact with the magnet.
- After the demonstration, explain the properties that made the magnet and the control material magnetically attracted. As the group goes down the line of other items, explain the properties these independent variables contained or lacked in terms of magnetism.
- Make sure to use the terminology you learned in your research to share and explain your findings.
- One way to ensure the appropriate terminology accompanies each step of the presentation is by using a slide show. As you progress through your presentation, the slide show can keep up, displaying the terms and definitions relevant to each item discussed. That way, the class can have a visual reminder for the topics you are discussing.

QUESTION: WHAT IMPACT WILL VARIABLES HAVE ON GRAVITATIONAL PULL?

The seventeenth-century English mathematician and physicist Sir Isaac Newton saw an apple fall from a tree and wondered why the apple dropped to the ground instead of going sideways or up. The answer is gravity, a natural force that attracts an item toward the center of the earth or toward another physical body or mass. Gravity affects all matter and is responsible for any two bodies of matter being attracted to each other, whether it's simply an apple falling to the

This 1905 painting by Robert Hannah depicts Isaac Newton near an apple tree, where he famously considered how gravity made an apple fall to the ground.

ground or the sun holding planets in its orbit. The larger the matter, the greater its gravity. That's why planets, moons, and stars have the greatest gravitational pull and why planets, such as Earth, powerfully draw objects toward their centers.

PROJECT
DEFYING GRAVITY

This group investigation will use variables to gain a better understanding of gravity.

- *Learn more about gravity. Research the experiments conducted by Galileo Galilei in the sixteenth and seventeenth centuries, Newton's apple incident, and the science to which they gave birth. Study the role of mass in gravity.*
- *Carry out a gravitational experiment using a pendulum, which in this case is a string hung on one end from a height, such as a desk or a lab table. On the loose end of the string, attach a weight, such as a block or a washer. Other tools, like a meterstick and a stopwatch, are helpful to accurately measure this experiment.*
- *Once the weight is attached to the loose end of the string, lift it on one side, keeping the string tight, and then release it. After the weight is released, it will swing back and forth for a while—sometimes for a long time. While it's swinging, observe the "period" of the pendulum. This is how long it takes for the weight to swing from one side to the other and back again.*

A meterstick (or yardstick), string, washers, and a stopwatch are all needed for this pendulum experiment to test gravitation pull.

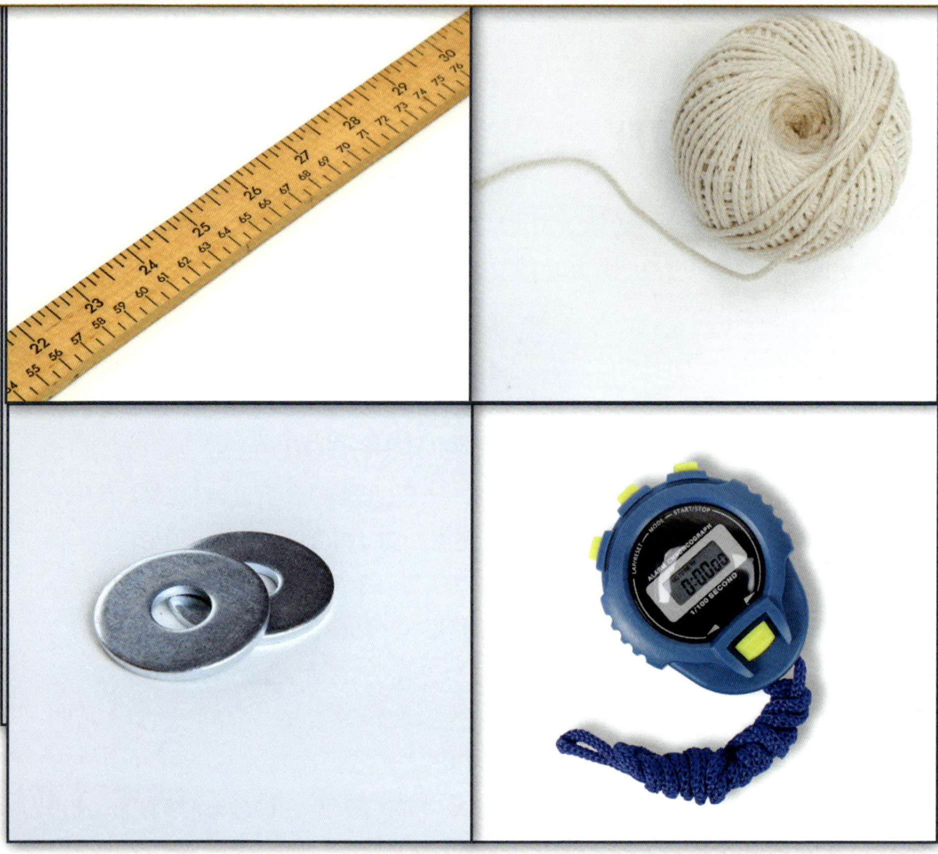

- *Record the weight of the object tied to the end of the string, the height or angle from which it was released, and the length of time of the period of the pendulum. Only by using that data can variables be accurately tested. To ensure accuracy, measure the period of the pendulum by letting it complete ten full*

cycles (a cycle is the process of swinging back and forth for a period), and then stop the pendulum. Add up the amount of time the pendulum took to complete ten full cycles, and then divide that number by ten. That gives the group an average period of the pendulum from which to base its experiment.

- *Next, hypothesize what factors could impact the period of the pendulum. The group can brainstorm ideas for this, but a simple starter hypothesis is that changing the amount of weight at the end of the string will impact the period of the pendulum. To study this hypothesis, remove the original item tied to the end of the string and replace it with an object of a different weight. For accuracy, take care to release the pendulum from the same angle or height that was used before. Measure the period with the new weight and compare the result to when the original weight was used. If the period changed when the weight was changed, the hypothesis was correct. If the period did not change when the weight was changed, the hypothesis did not stand up.*
- *Continue to experiment with independent variables. Make sure to record the procedures, hypotheses, observations, measurements, discussion, and conclusions throughout the experiment.*
- *When the group has concluded its experiment, record the data in a table*

accompanied by observations. This data will be helpful when the group presents its experiment to the class. The presentation can include a demonstration of the original period of the pendulum experiment to show the class how the control was determined. Then, the group can change variables to demonstrate how and if the independent variables impacted the period of the pendulum. In the group presentation, remember to use terminology relevant to the experiment and to the subject of gravity.

QUESTION: CAN CORROSION BE STOPPED OR SLOWED DOWN BY APPLYING A PROTECTIVE COATING TO METAL?

Have you ever seen a rusty nail, a rusty bucket, or metal that is so worn and rusty that it has holes? Perhaps you have handled a penny that looked dull and rusty. If so, what you observed was a scientific process called corrosion, which happens to some metals when they're exposed to elements like oxygen and water and become chemically unstable. Corrosion can be dangerous, especially when it occurs on bridges, on railroad tracks, and within other infrastructure. If a metal is too unstable due to corrosion, it may fail to do an important job.

PROJECT
CORROSION

Using variables, the group will expose metal to various elements to test corrosion.

- *Research corrosion and oxidization. Study the chemical elements involved in those processes, such as iron and oxygen, and the bonds that hold their molecules together.*
- *Assemble the materials: four brand-new metal nails, vegetable oil, acrylic paint, WD-40, four clear cups, and enough tap water to fill the clear cups to the same height.*
- *Hypothesize what the effect of oil, paint, and WD-40 will be on the rusting process.*
- *Prepare the nails. The first nail is the control. You don't need to do anything to it. It will interact only with oxygen and water. Coat the second nail with vegetable oil, the third nail with acrylic paint, and the fourth nail with WD-40. The nails that have been treated with vegetable oil, acrylic paint, and WD-40 are the experimental group. You will observe these nails to see if the substances applied*

Brand-new metal nails are a good starting point to study the corrosive effects of various substances.

to them—the independent variables—can impact or prevent corrosion.

- *Fill the clear plastic cups with water, and place each nail in its own cup.*
- *Allow the nails to sit in their cups of water for six or more days. Each day, observe what's happening to the nails. Specifically, note how the three treated nails are behaving compared to the untreated nail. Take photographic evidence of the nails every day and record written observations.*
- *Put together a presentation for the class. Using a presentation tool like PowerPoint, show the photos taken every day of the experiment to demonstrate the chemical processes the nails went through over the course of the experiment. Finally, reveal the group's findings: Did any of the treatments (vegetable oil, acrylic paint, and WD-40) prevent corrosion, when compared to the untreated nail? If so, by how much?*
- *After the presentation, properly dispose of the materials used in this experiment.*

CHAPTER TWO

LIFE SCIENCE

Have you ever questioned how a tiny seed can grow into a plant with leaves, stems, and fruits? If so, you've pondered life science, which is the study of organisms and the ways they interact with each other. Organisms fall on a wide spectrum, from microorganisms to plants to animals—including human beings. Everything from the food we eat to the practice of medicine and the use of fingerprints or DNA in police forensics involves life science.

QUESTION: WHAT EFFECT DOES LIGHT HAVE ON PLANT GROWTH?

To grow, plants need light. Some need a lot of light; some need only a little. Plants (and some other organisms, such as green algae) convert the energy from light into chemical energy that's stored up and released to fuel activity, such as growth. This process is called photosynthesis.

Photosynthesis does a lot more than help plants and organisms grow. It carries other heavy burdens: producing and maintaining

How light impacts plant life is evident in natural settings, such as forests, but it can also be explored using seedlings in the classroom.

the atmosphere's oxygen content and supplying all the organic compounds and much of the energy needed to maintain life on earth.

PROJECT
PHOTOSYNTHESIS

In this project, you will investigate photosynthesis by studying how varying light sources impact seed growth.

- *First, obtain three small planting pots of equal size, potting soil, and six seeds. Fast-growing seeds like sunflowers, morning glories, or beans are best. The seeds should all be for the exact same kind of plant.*
- *Research cellular function in plants and how cells support life functions. Determine the typical germination (growth) time for the seeds you selected, how much water the seeds should be given, and how often they should be watered.*
- *Select three distinct locations in the classroom for each of the three pots: a sunny*

place, like a windowsill (the seed placed in the windowsill will be the group's control group); a dark place, like a closet or beneath a desk; and a place that falls somewhere in between the first two places, like on a desk or a bookshelf. The dark location and the location in between darkness and light are the experimental group. The amount of light the plants get is the independent variable.

- *Next, it's time to form a hypothesis. How do you think light will impact the growth of the seeds?*
- *Then fill the three pots with equals amount of soil. In each pot, carefully push two seeds about half an inch (1.3 centimeters) into the soil and cover it up. It's important that the amount of*

PROJECT-BASED LEARNING

What's the role in project-based learning in science? PBL allows students to drive the project from beginning to end, as a project group. The group may need some help and direction from teachers, but PBL requires students to initiate, research, carry out, and present a project or experiment from beginning to end. PBL also encourages students to use technology like photos and video, presentation tools, software- or internet-based organization and collaboration tools, and software that helps track the milestones of a scientific experiment. Instead of being told what to learn, students find ways to learn on their own.

When planting seeds to study plant life, make sure the amount of soil and depth of planting is consistent across all pots.

soil and how deeply the seeds are planted are consistent across all three pots.

- *Place one pot in each of the locations selected during the project's research phase. Give each of the three pots a number or a name for recording purposes. For instance, Pot A can be the windowsill pot. Naming or numbering the pots will help clarify observations when you take notes and record data.*
- *Follow the directions for watering the seeds that you found in your research. Make sure each of the seeds gets exactly the same amount of water at the same exact frequency. Remember, the group is studying light's impact on growth. No other variables, such as unequal watering, should interfere.*
- *Record observations on each of the plants daily. It will take some time, maybe a week or more, for the seeds to sprout above the surface of the soil. Continue to observe the pots*

anyway to record and chronicle observations, chart progress by date, and take photos at various stages.

- *After at least one seed sprouts, continue to monitor the progress of all three pots. Tend to the seeds and/or sprouts with equal attention. After a few weeks, the group should be able to see how light impacts photosynthesis.*
- *Using a presentation tool, assemble data from the experiment and photographic evidence in a chronological sequence to demonstrate the seeds' growth in each of the three locations. When you make the presentation, walk your classmates through the various stages of growth and have each of the three pots out for the demonstration. Inform the class whether your hypothesis about light and growth was supported or contradicted. Remember to use the terminology that was learned during research and experimentation in the presentation so classmates can understand photosynthesis.*

QUESTION: HOW DOES SOIL PH IMPACT PLANT GROWTH?

Have you ever walked down a sidewalk and noticed that grass grows on one side but not on the other? Have you ever wondered why trees grow better in some places than in others? Maybe you've been to a home-goods store and noticed many kinds of potting and planting materials

The flowers of *Hydrangea macrophylla* are blue for plants that grow in acidic soil. However, plants of the same species that grow in alkaline soil have pink flowers.

for sale; some are for flowers, others for vegetables, and still others for growing grass. While many environmental and genetic factors are involved in plant growth, the various kinds of potting soil for sale give us a clue about how, where, and why plant life grows in some places but not others and why plants thrive in certain places over others. Certain types of soil are conditioned for certain types of growth. And when it comes to soil, what is most important is the pH—the acidity content of the soil. Soil pH is a defining factor in plant life. If a soil is too acidic (because of the presence of elements like aluminum, iron, or manganese), it can be toxic to some plants and restrict their growth.

PROJECT
SOIL PH AND PLANT GROWTH

In this project, a group will study the effect of changing the pH on grass growth.

- *Research soil pH and its related subjects, such as the numeric system on which pH is measured, how pH testing works, and what it means to have an acidic pH, neutral pH, or alkaline pH. The group will also explore how soil pH is related to factors such as oxidation, toxicity, water availability, and plant nutrients.*

- *Obtain twelve pots, potting soil, dirt, grass seeds, lime, aluminum sulfate, a pH measuring tool, water, and a ruler.*
- *Next, form a hypothesis based on the research. It should center on whether an acidic pH or an alkaline pH is better for plant growth or if neither are good for growth.*
- *Fill ten of the pots with a cup of potting soil each. Fill each of the other two pots with a cup of dirt from a different location, such as your schoolyard and your garden.*
- *Measure the pH of the potting soil in one of the pots and then set it aside. This will be your control. At this point, also measure the pH of the two pots with dirt.*
- *Then adjust the pH of the soil in the nine other potting-soil-filled pots by adding lime (which will make the soil more alkaline) or aluminum sulfate (which will make the soil more acidic). Mix in different amounts of lime or aluminum sulfate (or combine the two), testing the soil's pH after you mix each batch. You want to end up with a range of pH levels between 5.0 and 9.0. A pH of 7.0 is neutral, so this will give you some variety to work with.*

Testing the soil pH in your experiment is key to understanding how this measurement impacts growth patterns.

- *Label each pot with its pH level and any variables added to it, such as the lime or aluminum sulfate. On the two pots of dirt, note where the dirt came from.*
- *Add twenty grass seeds to each pot.*
- *Place the twelve pots in a place where they'll all receive equal access to sunlight. Water each pot daily, making sure to water each pot with the exact same amount of water.*

- *Over the next three weeks, check on the grass every other day. During that time, note how many, if any, of the grass seeds have sprouted, what color the sprouts are, and how long the smallest and largest blades of grass are.*
- *Note also how the grass planted in the two pots of dirt fares compared to the grass in the ten pots of potting soil. Take notes and photos to chronicle the grass's growth.*
- *Use a presentation tool to assemble the observations and photographic evidence in chronological order. When presenting to the class, have all twelve pots out so class members can see the experiment's results for themselves. In the presentation, use terminology learned during the group's research so the entire class can learn from the experiment. Use the presentation to hold a class discussion of the environmental factors that may change the pH of the soil we rely on to grow food and support plant life.*

QUESTION: ARE FINGERPRINTS INHERITED?

If you've ever pressed your thumb against a glass window, into clay, or even into Play-Doh, you left something behind: a fingerprint. A fingerprint is formed by ridges in the skin; these ridges provide friction, allowing us to grasp items. Everybody's ridge patterns are unique, but they generally fall into one of three patterns: a whorl, a loop, or an arch. Some people have just one of these patterns. Others have two or all three.

Arches, loops, and whorls are aspects of our fingerprints that make every individual's fingerprint a unique indicator of their DNA.

Fingerprints are an expression of our DNA, a molecule that holds our genetic code. These molecules are mostly found in the nuclei of our cells—and every human has between thirty and forty trillion cells! That means every individual's DNA is held within trillions of tiny cells. Between any two people, about 99.9 percent of their DNA is the same. The remaining one-tenth of 1 percent is what makes us unique. A person's DNA is mostly inherited from his or her parents. This helps explain why some of us look so much like our family members. But does that explanation extend to fingerprints?

PROJECT
FINGERPRINTS AND DNA

Unlike many other projects, this one starts with an experiment rather than research. Once your data is collected through the experiment, the group will research to understand the data and confirm or deny the hypothesis: are fingerprints inherited?

To make comparisons about fingerprints, at least two group members will need to get fingerprints from a sibling, a parent, or other blood relative, all of whom must provide signed consent to participate.

- *To begin, form a hypothesis about whether fingerprints have a genetic basis.*
- *Collect the group members' fingerprints. Use the following method:*
  - *First, rub a pencil on a piece of blank white paper to form and fill in a box of about 1 × 1 inch (3 × 3 cm).*
  - *Then, clean your hands and thoroughly dry them with a paper towel. Press the right index fingertip, sliding slightly to each side, over the penciled-in box on the paper. Your fingertip will be coated with graphite dust.*
  - *Press your fingertip onto the sticky side of a piece of clear tape. Then attach the tape to a piece of white paper. The fingerprint should be visible on the tape, against the white background of the paper. The group can practice this until the fingerprints are clearly visible each time.*
  - *Make sure everyone who provides a fingerprint has a brand-new penciled-in box to use. If multiple people use the same penciled-in box, there will not be enough graphite dust for a good print, and the data will not be accurate.*
- *Label the fingerprint samples by name or by number. If the samples are not identified by name, keep a record of who contributed which*

fingerprint. After the group members have all provided fingerprints, take the time to examine them. How different are they? How similar are they? Is it hard to tell one from another?

- *Next, a few group members should collect the fingerprints of a sibling, parent, or other blood relative. Use the same methods you used to collect group members' fingerprints, and don't forget to collect signed consent forms.*
- *After the fingerprints of family members have been collected, examine the results. Do any of the group members who fingerprinted members of their families have the same exact fingerprint as their family members? How does that information impact the hypothesis the group formed about whether fingerprints are inherited?*
- *Now it's time to research why the group's hypothesis was supported or contradicted. There's a lot of interesting information on DNA and, specifically, on fingerprint DNA. This research can help the group understand what it discovered upon comparison of each other's fingerprints and the fingerprints of family members against the group members who collected them. As the group researches and learns more about fingerprint DNA, revisit the fingerprints themselves to see if any patterns are inherited.*
- *Find a creative way to present the fingerprints of both group members and family members*

A student examines fingerprint evidence after a police demonstration about an investigation. Because every person's fingerprints are unique, fingerprints aid police in identifying suspects.

to the class. Remember to place the family members' fingerprints next to the group member who is related to them. The fingerprints on display should be the visual element of the group's presentation, while the group explains the experiment and its findings. Remember to use terminology learned during the research so that classmates can understand and learn from what you're showing and telling them.

CHAPTER THREE

EARTH AND SPACE SCIENCE

You've looked up and seen the stars. You've looked around and seen land, water, and life systems. Did you know that what you see in the sky and what you see around you on earth are all connected? They are. One way you can see this is in earth's cycles, including the water, rock, carbon, and nitrogen cycle, as well as in the moon's lunar cycle. These systems constantly change, shape, impact, and sustain life on earth. What you see right in front of you when you're outdoors and what you see far away in the sky form a very special relationship: the scientific discipline of earth and space science. While both have been studied for centuries and we've even put a man on the moon, both earth and space contain vast unknowns, even for the most brilliant scientists.

QUESTION: HOW DOES ACID RAIN DAMAGE PLANT LIFE?

Acid rain … sounds scary, right? That's because it is. Acid rain is rainfall that has been made acidic by pollution. This kind of rain causes harm to the environment, especially to forests and lakes. It's mostly caused by the industrial use and burning of fossil fuels, which produce waste gases that contain sulfur and nitrogen oxides. When these gases combine with water, you get acid rain. Because it can fall on vast swaths of forest and bodies of water, acid rain has an enormous global impact.

This spruce forest in the Czech Republic was severely damaged by acid rain, which is a type of super-polluted precipitation.

PROJECT
ACID RAIN

In this experiment, the group will mimic the effects of acid rain on the environment. The group will also investigate how liquids of varying acidities (pH) impact plant growth.

- *Gather the necessary materials for the experiment: four large jars, distilled water, white vinegar, measuring cups, a stirring spoon, and plant cuttings. Each of the plant cuttings should consist of one leaf and a small amount of a stem. You'll want four cuttings each from*

A coleus plant, like the one pictured here, provides good stem and leaf cuttings for fast-growing plants like the ones you'll need to study acid rain.

two different types of plants. Cuttings from a philodendron plant and either a begonia or coleus plant, which all have fast-growing roots, are recommended, but you can discuss replacement plants with a teacher if you have trouble finding those species.

- *While the experiment's materials are being obtained, conduct research about acid rain. Learn more about the chemical and biological components that combine in the atmosphere to create acid rain, where acid rain is most common, and what causes it. During the research, keep an eye out for solutions to acid rain.*
- *Fill all four of the jars with water. Make sure to put the same amount of water in each jar. Using the measuring cups, add varying amounts of the white vinegar to three of the jars and stir it in. The jar without the vinegar is the control. The amount of vinegar mixed into the water in the other jars is the*

THE HUMAN FACTOR

Why is it important to study the environment and subjects like acid rain and climate change? Because human interference has caused irreversible damage to our natural environment through the continued use of finite, polluting resources like petroleum gasoline; through large-scale industrialization; through overpopulation; and through the destruction of some of earth's greatest resources, like open space and rain forests. Earth science gives us the chance to examine the environmental problems we face on a global scale. Every single person on our planet is in peril if we don't find solutions to these problems.

independent variable in this project, so be sure to record how much vinegar is added to each of the three jars.

- *Add one plant cutting of each type of plant to each of the four jars.*
- *Based on what you have learned in your research, form a hypothesis about the damage the cuttings might sustain based on the level of acidity they're subjected to in the jars.*
- *Over the next two weeks, observe the cuttings in each of the four jars. Document observations by charting growth, the appearance of the cuttings, and how much time has passed since the cuttings were placed in the jars. Note the differences not only between the control and the plants with vinegar but also between the cuttings subjected to varying*

amounts of vinegar. Note whether the vinegar had a stronger effect on one type of plant than on the other. Take photos throughout the two-week observation period to document appearance.

- *The group's presentation to the class should include the photographic evidence of the impact that the contents of all four jars had on the cuttings. Display the charts you made to document the plants' growth and appearance. (You could even make graphs to present this data.) Make sure the jars themselves, with the cuttings, are on hand to present to the class. Reveal whether the group's hypothesis was upheld or not upheld. Drawing on the efforts to prevent to acid rain that the group discovered in its research, lead a discussion with the class about acid rain and its impact on earth and its atmosphere.*

QUESTION: WHAT IS GLOBAL WARMING? HOW CAN WE DEMONSTRATE ITS EFFECTS?

You've probably heard of global warming. This is the rise in temperatures at earth's surface and in the lower atmosphere over roughly the past hundred years. Scientists attribute global warming to something called the greenhouse effect.

In a greenhouse, short-wave radiation—in the form of sunlight—passes through the glass and is converted to long-wave radiation—in the form of heat—that can't pass back out again. The greenhouse also becomes humid because the heat causes evaporation, which also cannot escape through the windows. This makes a greenhouse a warm and moist environment for growing plants, which is especially needed in cold or dry areas.

Certain gases in our atmosphere—which are logically, if somewhat unimaginatively, known as greenhouse gases—behave the same way that the glass does in a greenhouse. These gases trap heat inside the atmosphere, and it is thanks to them that earth is warm enough for life as we know it to exist. Some of

This image shows the greenhouse effect, a natural process that warms the earth—but also one that is accelerated and exacerbated by human activity, causing destructive global warming.

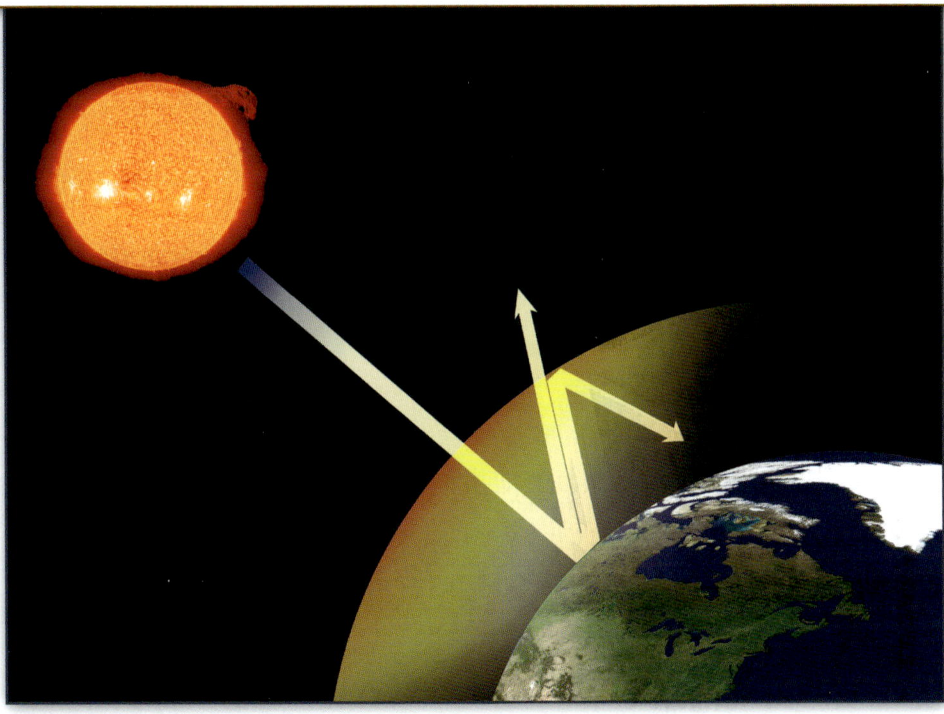

the greenhouse gas in the atmosphere is the result of natural events, such as volcanoes erupting. However, human activities have significantly increased the amount of these gases in the atmosphere over the past few centuries. This sudden spike in greenhouse gases is trapping more heat than in the past, causing temperatures to rise. The increase in global warming disrupts our climates, causes floods and major storms like hurricanes, and destroys the habitats of many species.

One way to think about the greenhouse effect is to consider what it has in common with evaporation, the process by which water is turned to vapor. For instance, a pot of boiling water covered with a lid will only continue to get hotter and produce more warmth and condensation. A pot of boiling water without a lid, however, can allow for evaporation, and therefore it won't produce the same extreme heat and condensation as the lidded pot. What's happening with global warming is, in simple terms, the pot of boiling water with a lid on it.

PROJECT
EVAPORATION AND GLOBAL WARMING

Using a simple experiment about evaporation, you can mimic the greenhouse effect and see for yourself what happens when gases can't find their way back out.

- *The project should begin with research on evaporation and global warming. Using what you learn, form a hypothesis about what will happen when one jar of water is left uncovered and one is covered with aluminum foil.*

- *To carry out the experiment, you'll need aluminum foil, two identical jars, and water.*
- *Fill the two jars with equal amounts of water. Leave one uncovered (it will be your control) and cover the other with aluminum foil (the foil will be the independent variable). Place them outside in an equally sunny spot. You could instead pick a sunny spot inside, like a windowsill. To expand on this experiment, thermometers can be placed in the water so that temperature can be tracked alongside evaporation.*

Observing the items in your experiments and taking photographic evidence of the project's phases are key in presenting your findings to your teacher and classmates.

- *Take a picture of the jars. Then measure and record their current water levels at the time of placement. Return every day for a week to observe, take a photo, and measure the water level of each jar.*
- *After a week, conclude the experiment and note the results. When placed in an equally*

sunny spot, what happened to the water levels? Prepare a presentation for your class, including a slide show of the week's worth of photos chronicling the water's progress in the sun, accompanied by charts and written explanations. Make sure to note the difference between the water in the uncovered jar and the water in the jar that was covered by aluminum foil.

- *Make your presentation to the class. Reveal whether the hypothesis was correct. Then explain how the evaporation experiment works as a metaphor for global warming. Lead a class discussion about global warming and why it's an important topic for people to understand. As a class, brainstorm other creative ways to teach about this environmental problem.*

CHAPTER FOUR

ENGINEERING DESIGN

Unlike the other projects in this text, which rely heavily on scientific experiments and observation to test a theory, engineering design involves designing, building, and testing something to see if it can meet a certain expectation. Engineers and their techniques are integral to our everyday lives, from the way devices work in our houses to the cars we drive to the rockets we send into space. Engineers imagine how to solve a problem and build something to fill a need.

QUESTION: CAN A NATURAL, RENEWABLE SOURCE OF ENERGY WORK TO TAKE THE PLACE OF A NONRENEWABLE FOSSIL FUEL?

Due to global warming, environmental concerns, and the push toward sustainability, lots of people are seeking alternatives to gasoline to power their vehicles and tools. Gasoline is made from the fossil fuel petroleum. Petroleum is a finite resource, and it's nonrenewable. This means that, unlike solar or wind

Most drivers rely on petroleum gasoline to fuel their cars. Unfortunately, this type of fuel is a finite resource, and it has a harmful effect on the environment.

power, it can get used up, and unlike lumber or crops, it can't be replanted. Burning gasoline also has harmful environmental impacts, and humans use it faster than it can be produced.

Seeing the danger in relying on petroleum gasoline, engineers and activists have been trying to find alternatives. In fact, singer, songwriter, and environmental activist Willie Nelson motors around in a bus fueled by a biodiesel combination of soybean and vegetable oils, rather than traditional gasoline. Battery-charged cars have become all the rage among the environmentally conscious. This begs the question: can traditional fossil fuels finally be replaced?

SUSTAINABILITY

Sustainability has become a popular word among advocates for the environment, architects, builders, and engineers. At a basic level, sustainability refers to how a biological species survives. On a larger scale, it refers to whether certain actions can be carried out without permanent and harmful changes to the environment. For humans and all species, sustainability is necessary to secure our physical well-being. For mechanics, engineers, and the structures humans produce, it refers to increasing reliability while also conserving resources. Sustainable practices, like engineering, are necessary to ensure a future in which we haven't destroyed all of earth's precious resources. For those with a mind for science, design, mechanics, building, and engineering, the future is bright with opportunities as society moves toward sustainable practices. However, everyone should practice sustainability by doing small things like recycling, reusing, and reducing waste.

PROJECT
BURNING FUEL

A renewable alternative to gasoline, such as vegetable oil or another biofuel, could help save our natural resources and cut down on pollutants. The experiment will use equivalent amounts of one nonrenewable fuel and three agro fuels (such as vegetable oil) to measure the heat produced by the different fuels.

NOTE: This project requires adult supervision, safety equipment, and a well-ventilated area away from combustibles and flammables.

- *Start by researching various energy sources (specifically nonrenewable and renewable energy sources) and how different energy sources produce heat. Make sure the research includes what heat energy (how much energy a source generates when used) demonstrates about a fuel source.*
- *Obtain the materials for this project:*
    - *Four large paper clips (metal, not coated with any material)*
    - *Clothesline or cotton cord, cut into four pieces of about 1 inch (3 cm) each*
    - *Four ring stands and ring clamps, or four wire coat hangers bent to provide a makeshift ring stand*
    - *Four soda cans (cleaned, with metal tabs removed) or four tin cans*
    - *Four foam cups*
    - *Four scientific thermometers*
    - *One container of motor oil, #20 or #30 (an*

Testing motor oil against vegetable oil is one way we can learn whether biofuels, such as vegetable oil, can be viable alternatives to traditional petroleum gasoline.

alternative to motor oil is liquefied coal from a true coal sample, which can be found on some online science stores)

- *Vegetable oil, peanut oil, and another biofuel option, such as safflower oil*
- *Ruler, scissors, stopwatch, lab notebook, and graph paper (graph paper can be replaced by a digital resource, like Excel)*

- Fireplace or grill lighter
- Glass eyedropper
- Cold water and graduated cylinder that will let you measure 100 milliliters of water
- Camera or video camera to record the experiment

- Hypothesize which of the four materials has more heat energy. Record it in your notebook.
- On the graph paper (or using software instead of graph paper), draw a comparison chart. Along the y-axis (the vertical line), create a column titled "Oil Tested" and list each oil the group will test. Along the x-axis (the horizontal line), create three separate columns: the first column titled "Temperature of Cold Water," the second column titled "Temperature After Burning," and the third column titled "Difference in Temperature."
- Bend each paper clip so it has a circular base and one end propped up, vertically. The paper clips should be able to stand on their own.
- On each paper clip's vertical length, vertically thread one of the 1-inch (3 cm) clothesline or cotton cord pieces.
- Saturate each piece of clothesline or cotton cord with an equivalent amount of the oils being tested; a good way to do this is to saturate each with twenty drops of oil using the eyedropper.

- *Using the measuring cup, fill all four soda or tin cans with 100 milliliters of cold water.*
- *Cover each of the cans with a foam cup, bottom side up; the upside-down foam cup should rest against the top rim of the can.*
- *Poke a thermometer into each of the foam cups. Make sure the thermometers are in the water but not touching the cans. You might need to use tape to secure the thermometers in the correct position.*
- *Measure the temperature of the cold water and record it on the comparison chart.*
- *Suspend each of the cans from the ring stands or the coat hanger frame.*
- *Place the clothesline or cotton cord, propped up on the paper clips, under each can.*
- *Let an adult light the clothesline or cotton cord saturated with motor oil. Let the oil burn completely and, in the comparison chart, record the water temperature. This is the control. (Remember to get a photo or take video of this step!)*
- *Have the adult light each of the other three clothesline or cotton cord pieces that are saturated with the bio oils, allowing each oil to burn completely. (Remember to get photos or video of each!)*
- *Once each oil has burned completely, record the water temperature on the comparison chart.*

- *Calculate the differences in the temperatures and record on the comparison chart.*
- *Relying on your research, discuss what the results mean. Did any of the renewable sources perform as well or nearly as well as the motor oil? How do the results support or refute the hypothesis?*
- *Assemble a presentation that includes yours hypothesis, the materials used, pictures or video of each of the oil lightings, and the results. Finally, the presentation should inform the class whether renewable energy sources can potentially replace nonrenewable sources.*

QUESTION: CAN HUMAN-MADE DEVICES DO THE JOB OF A HUMAN ARM?

Whether in a comic book, on television, in movies, or even in real life, we've all seen robots. Robotics is a field of engineering design in which scientists have explored nearly every facet of human life—in robotic form. War veterans who've lost limbs now have the use of replacements with robotic components. Self-driving cars exist. Every year brings more experimentation and refinement in the field of robotics. The field itself perfectly encapsulates the field of engineering design: of imagining something, designing it, building it, and testing it until it reaches a point at which it's useful, either to replace or enhance a human function.

These engineering students are experimenting with a trebuchet—or medieval-style catapult—to mechanically launch a tennis ball. The ball went 89 feet (27 meters).

PROJECT
BALL LAUNCH

In this group project, a team will apply the principles of physics and engineering through mechanics. The group will build a launcher device to throw a ball as far as possible, as well as a receiver to catch it. The receiver adds some challenge to a traditional catapult project. In developing multiple designs, testing the launcher and catcher designs, and modifying them, the group will demonstrate the engineering design process.

- *To begin this project, research similar projects, as well as the principles of simple physics, mechanics, and engineering. The website for the organization Science Buddies is one source to consult. Also check out the Fluor Engineering Challenge and the PBS Kids Design Squad site: http://pbskids.org/designsquad/project/11379/.*
- *Think about what items can be used to construct the launcher and receiver using a set of materials that are readily available—cups, rulers, tape, a ball of aluminum foil, and other everyday objects. Discuss ideas with your teammates and work together to come up with a launcher and receiver design. Then build the two machines.*
- *Before testing the machine, come up with a hypothesis about whether the launcher and receiver the group constructs is indeed capable of matching the ability of the human arm.*
- *To test your hypothesis, you will need to establish your control by figuring out how far the students can throw a ball and how often*

and accurately the ball is caught by another student. Remember to record that data.

- *Run multiple trials with the launcher and receiver in this project. Don't forget to add variables by modifying and perfecting the design of the launcher and receiver. Always record data and take photographic or video evidence that the group can present to the class during its presentation.*
- *Put together a presentation about your investigation. Inform the class whether the group's hypothesis was supported. Explain what modifications were most successful and discuss why. Come up with a creative way to cover the material, such as making a movie about it or putting on a series of dramatic outdoor demonstrations.*

USEFUL TOOLS

Project-based learning encourages the use of technology that helps students research their ideas, organize project assets, collaborate, and create products of all kinds. Rely on tools to store information, share with the group and teachers, and create a product for the end presentation. Use collaborative tools that permit access outside of school for the individual student, the group, and the teacher, since the project may involve homework.

Below are helpful project-based learning applications. All of them are free, offer free subscriptions, or have free trial versions. Obtain teacher approval of any tools used in a project.

- **Research:** Britannica School, Google (especially Google Scholar), Todoist, EndNote, Digital Public Library of America, Citelighter, SweetSearch, Diigo
- **News:** CNN Student News, Newseum, KQED, Smithsonian's TweenTribune, *PBS NewsHour* Extra
- **Organization, Collaboration, and Communication:** Stormboard, Google Drive and Hangouts, Evernote, Slack, Pinterest, LiveBinders, Asana
- **Science Tools:** Cells Alive!, ChemCollective, Climate Zone.com, Chemicool, Concord Consortium, ElectroCity, Global Warming Interactive, Google Earth, Google Sky, Impact: Earth, Learn.Genetics, My Footprint.org, NASA Education, Ocean in Google Earth, Periodic Table of Videos, Scitable, Teach the Earth (https://serc.carleton.edu/teachearth/index.html)
- **Map Tools:** Animaps, EChalk Interactive Earth, PictraMap, Google Earth, TimeMap, Globe for iPad, Cesium WebGL Virtual Globe, Earth 3D—Amazing Atlas
- **Mind and Concept Mapping:** Mindomo, MindMap, MindMeister

- **Posters, Multimedia, and Publishing:** Glogster, Issuu, Scrivener
- **Digital Presentation/Project Portfolios:** Pathbrite, Google Slides, PowerPoint, PresentationTube, Prezi
- **Website Creation and Blogging:** Google Sites, Duda, Wikispaces, WordPress, Weebly, Wix, SnapPages, Sitey, StudentShow, Yola
- **Video:** YouTube, iMovie, LifeLogger, WeVideo, Magisto, TeleStory
- **Animation, Drawing, and Infographics:** Typrorama, Do Ink, Piktochat, Pixabay, Freepik
- **Podcasts:** GarageBand, Audacity
- **Survey/Feedback:** Survey Monkey, Google Forms

GLOSSARY

acid A sour substance with a pH of under 7.

alkaline A state in which a substance (as a hydroxide) neutralizes acids.

biofuels Fuels designed to replace gasoline that are made mostly from plants that have just been harvested.

control Also known as a control group, the group (or single example) in an experiment that is not exposed to the object or effect that the person doing the experiment is testing.

corrosion The process in which metal is eaten away and becomes chemically unstable.

DNA Short for "deoxyribonucleic acid"; the molecule that contains the genetic code of organisms.

electron A tiny particle that has a negative charge and travels around the nucleus, or center, of an atom.

ferromagnetic Relating to substances (as iron and nickel) that are easily magnetized.

fossil fuels Energy sources, such as oil, coal, and natural gas, that are the remains of organisms that lived long ago.

genetic Relating to genes, which are the way in which traits are passed down from parents to their offspring.

matter The substance of which a physical object is composed.

nonrenewable Derived from natural resources that cannot be replaced after they are used.

organism An individual living thing, such as a plant, fungus, or animal.

oxidization The process of going through a chemical reaction that involves losing electrons to another substance. This happens to many substances when they react with oxygen.

pendulum A body hung from a fixed point so as to swing freely back and forth under the action of gravity.

pH A number used in expressing acidity or alkalinity on a scale whose values run from 0 to 14, with 7 representing neutrality, numbers less than 7 increasing acidity, and numbers greater than 7 increasing alkalinity.

photosynthesis The process by which plants that contain chlorophyll make carbohydrates from water and from carbon dioxide in the air in the presence of light.

physics A science that deals with matter and energy and their actions on each other in the fields of mechanics, heat, light, electricity, sound, and the atomic nucleus.

species A type of living thing. All human beings are one species.

sustainability Development that meets the needs of the present without compromising the ability of future generations to meet their own needs.

variable A quantity that may take on any one of a set of values.

FOR MORE INFORMATION

Buck Institute for Education (BIE)
3 Hamilton Landing, Suite 220
Novato, CA 94949
(415) 883-0122
Website: http://www.bie.org
Facebook and Twitter: @biepbl
YouTube: @BIEPBL
The BIE is a premier resource for project-based learning initiatives and resources. Its PBL pages provide ideas and rubrics that students can use to predict and shape their performance, planning forms, and research.

Canadian Association for the Advancement of Science
3034 Edgemont Blvd.
North Vancouver, BC V7R 4X1
Canada
Website: http://caas-acascience.org
The Canadian Association for the Advancement of Science is a nonprofit with the mission of encouraging people to learn about science and its impact on their lives by making information accessible and easy to understand. The organization also helps people of all ages understand the connections between science, technology, and society.

National Academy of Sciences
2101 Constitution Ave. NW
Washington, DC 20418
(202) 334-2000
Website: http://www.nasonline.org
Facebook, Instagram, Twitter, and YouTube: @theNASciences
Founded in 1863 by act of the US Congress, the National Academy of Sciences is a private, nonprofit society that provides independent, objective advice to the entire nation on science and technology. The organization furthers science in America through research and other activities to solve problems and inform public policy.

National Geographic
215 E. Sixty-Seventh St.

New York, NY 10065
Website: http://national geographic.org/education
Facebook, Instagram, and Twitter: @NatGeo
National Geographic is a longtime, world-renowned educational resource for the latest discoveries in science, animals, adventure, and the environment. National Geographic captures some of the world's most significant natural phenomena, from the study of the tiniest atoms and insects to research and documentation on entire populations.

National Research Council Canada
1200 Montreal Rd., Building M-58
Ottawa, ON K1A 0R6
Canada
(613) 993-9101
Website: https://www.nrc-cnrc.gc.ca/eng/index.html
Twitter: @NRC_CNRC
YouTube: @researchcouncilcan
The National Research Council is the Canadian government's primary research and development organization. The National Research Council maintains the National Science Library, manages multiple research and development programs, and upholds standards for ethics and integrity in science.

Science Buddies
Contact: scibuddy@sciencebuddies.org
Website: https://www.sciencebuddies.org
Facebook and Twitter: @ScienceBuddies
Science Buddies is a nonprofit organization that helps students from kindergarten through twelfth grade, parents, and teachers find science project ideas. Science Buddies not only helps users find science projects but makes available actual science teachers and experts to answer questions.

yourgenome
Contact: comment@yourgenome.org
Website: https://www.yourgenome.org
Facebook and Twitter: @yourgenome
YouTube: @yourgenome
Yourgenome is a website that allows visitors to find out everything they want to know about DNA, genes, and genomes. Visitors can find out what a genome is and how DNA is sequenced. The site helps learners explore what genetics say about an individual or a population and also introduces learners to the ethical questions and debates related to the study of DNA.

Youth Science Canada
1550 Kingston Rd., Suite 213
Pickering, ON L1V 1C3
Canada
(416) 341-0040
Website: https://www.youthscience.ca
Facebook: @ysc.sjc
Twitter and Instagram: @ysc_sjc
YouTube: @YOUTHSCIENCECANADA
Youth Science Canada is the nation's leading organization helping youths engage with science through inquiry and critical thinking. The organization is accredited under Imagine Canada's national standards program and helps students conduct science projects and understand ethics and values involved in scientific exploration.

FOR FURTHER READING

Bayden, Maya. *Earth Science* (The Study of Science). New York, NY: Britannica Educational Publishing, 2017.

Canavan, Thomas. *Growth and Development: Cells and DNA* (How Your Body Works). New York, NY: PowerKids Press, 2016.

Claybourne, Anna. *What Do You Know About Life Cycles?* (Test Your Science Skills). New York, NY: PowerKids Press, 2016.

Craig, Joe. *Safeguarding Water and Food Supplies* (Science to the Rescue: Adapting to Climate Change). New York, NY: Rosen Central, 2013.

Curley, Robert. *Renewable and Alternative Energy* (Energy: Past, Present, and Future). New York, NY: Britannica Educational Publishing, 2012.

Einspruch, Andrew. *DNA Detectives* (Discovery Education: Technology). New York, NY: PowerKids Press, 2013.

Kuhtz, Russell. *Physical Science* (The Study of Science). New York, NY: Britannica Educational Publishing, 2017.

Landon, Melissa. *Biology: Understanding Living Matter* (The Study of Science). New York, NY: Britannica Educational Publishing, 2015.

Mack, Molly. *Reducing Global Warming* (Global Guardians). New York, NY: PowerKids Press, 2017.

Royston, Angela. *The Race to Survive Climate Change* (World in Crisis). New York, NY: Rosen Central, 2015.

Spilsbury, Louise, and Richard Spilsbury. *Top 10 Worst Hurricanes* (Nature's Ultimate Disasters). New York, NY: PowerKids Press, 2017.

Vescia, Monique. *Engineers at Work* (Scientists at Work). New York, NY: Britannica Educational Publishing, 2018.

BIBLIOGRAPHY

Brubaker, Jack. "How to Calculate the Period of Pendulum." Sciencing, April 24, 2014. http://sciencing.com/calculate-period-pendulum-8194276.html.

Buck Institute for Education. "Why Project Based Learning (PBL)?" Retrieved April 17, 2018. http://www.bie.org/about/why_pbl.

Edutopia. "Getting Started with Project-Based Learning (Hint: Don't Go Crazy)." August 6, 2012. https://www.edutopia.org/blog/project-based-learning-getting-started-basics-andrew-miller.

Gibbens, Sarah. "Heart-Wrenching Video Shows Starving Polar Bear on Iceless Land." *National Geographic*, December 7, 2017. http://news.nationalgeographic.com/2017/12/polar-bear-starving-arctic-sea-ice-melt-climate-change-spd.

Jones, Anna Katherine. "What Makes Ice Melt Faster?" Prezi, November 13, 2013. https://prezi.com/wudydlfzmko0/what-makes-ice-melt-faster.

Mathaisel, Dennis F. X., et al. *Engineering for Sustainability*. Boca Raton, FL: CRC Press, 2013.

Nelson, Daniel. "What an Experimental Control Is and Why It's So Important." Science Trends, January 26, 2018. https://sciencetrends.com/experimental-control-important.

Next Generation Science Standards. "Read the Standards." http://www.nextgenscience.org/search-standards?keys=&tid%5B%5D=106&tid_3%5B%5D=97&=Submit.

Office for Coastal Management. "Impacts of Climate Change." National Oceanic and Atmospheric Administration. http://coast.noaa.gov.

Pellegrino, James W., et al. *Developing Assessments for the Next Generation Science Standards*. Washington, DC: National Academies Press, 2014.

Randall, Alex. "We Know Climate Is Going to Create Disaster Displacement—but How?" Climate and Migration Coalition, November 17, 2017. http://climatemigration.org.uk/placing-climate-change-amongst-the-causes-of-disasters.

Science Buddies. "Variables in Your Science Fair Project." Retrieved April 17, 2018. www.sciencebuddies.org/science-fair-projects/science-fair/variables.

Wellcome Genome Campus. "What Is a DNA Fingerprint?" June 2, 2016. http://www.yourgenome.org/facts/what-is-a-dna-fingerprint.

Yale Peabody Museum of Natural History. "Global Warming in a Jar." Retrieved April 17, 2018. http://peabody.yale.edu/sites/default/files/documents/education/Global%20Warming%20In%20A%20Jar.pdf.

INDEX

ABOUT THE AUTHOR

Angie Timmons studied journalism and sociology at Texas Tech University. She's worked in news writing and reporting, technical writing, marketing, and content management for companies in Austin and Dallas-Fort Worth and as a media consultant for two congressional campaigns. She has written several other titles for Rosen: *The Nanjing Massacre*, *Everything You Need to Know About Racism*, *Real-World Projects to Explore the Cold War*, *Real-World Projects to Explore World War II*, and *How to Create Digital Portfolios to Show What You Know*. She lives in a Dallas suburb with her husband, Jason, and their three cats.

PHOTO CREDITS

Cover, p. 1 Nicholas Prior/The Image Bank/Getty Images; p. 3 Ollyy/Shutterstock .com; p. 4 Pressmaster/Shutterstock.com; p. 6 Ableimages/DigitalVision/Getty Images; p. 10 Rubberball/Mike Kemp/Getty Images; p. 12 The Royal Institution, London, UK/Bridgeman Images; p. 14 (ruler) LesPalnik/Shutterstock.com, (string) Raihana Asral/Shutterstock.com, (stopwatch) PrimaStockPhoto/Shutterstock .com, (washers) Alexander Lukatskiy/Shutterstock.com; p. 17 Roman Sigaev /Shutterstock.com; p. 20 Hero Images/Getty Images; pp. 22, 42 Lisa F. Young /Shutterstock.com; p. 24 kai keisuke/Shutterstock.com; p. 26 blickwinkel/Alamy Stock Photo; p. 28 Arkadiusz Fajer/Shutterstock.com; p. 31 ZUMA Press Inc /Alamy Stock Photo; p. 33 Richard Packwood/Oxford Scientific/Getty Images; p. 34 Alina Kupstova/Shutterstock.com; p. 37 Monica Schroeder/Science Source; p. 39 BigLike Images/Shutterstock.com; p. 45 (motor oil) Konstantin Faratinov /Shutterstock.com, (vegetable oil) Andrey Eremin/Shutterstock.com; p. 49 Cyrus McCrimmon/Denver Post/Getty Images.

Design: Nelson Sá; Layout: Ellina Litmanovich; Editor: Amelie von Zumbusch; Photo Researcher: Karen Huang